In memory of my son, Rey.
Al-Fatihah.

Narrated by Abu Huraira:

Allah has ninety-nine Names, i.e., one hundred minus one, and whoever believes in their meanings and acts accordingly, will enter Paradise; and Allah is Witr (one) and loves 'the Witr' (i.e., odd numbers).

Sahih Bukhari, Vol. 8, Book 75, Hadith 419

الرحمان
Ar-Rahmaan
The Most Gracious

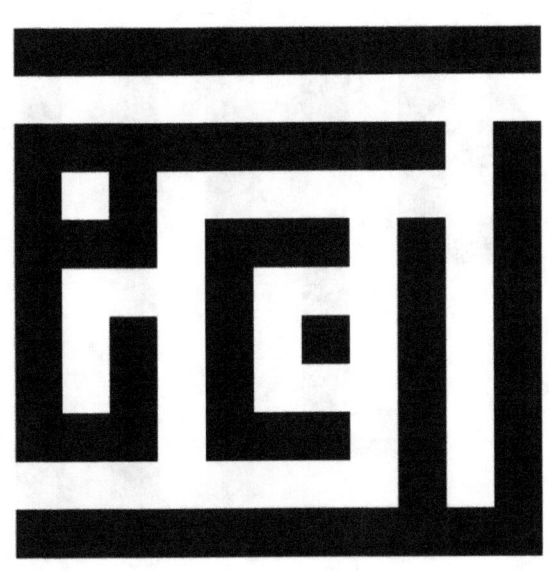

الرحيم

Ar-Raheem
The Most Merciful

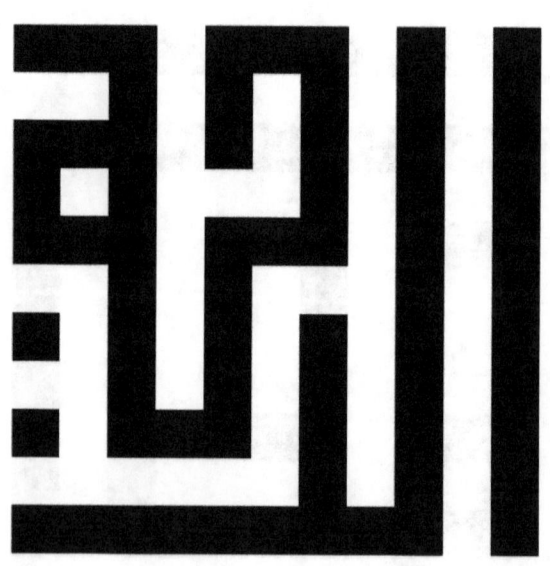

المـالك
Al-Maalik
The Supreme Lord

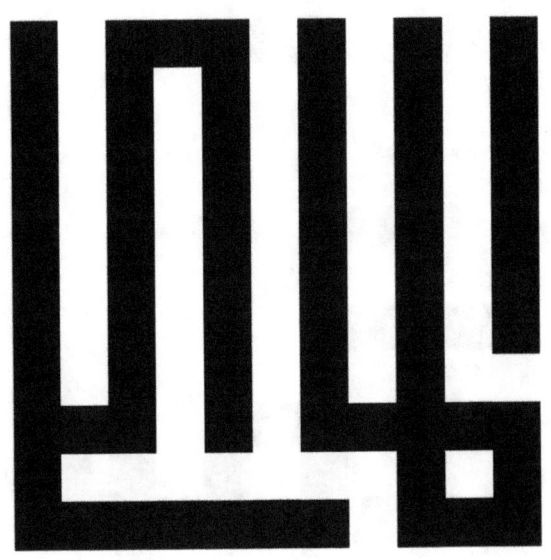

القدوس
Al-Quddoos
The All-Holy

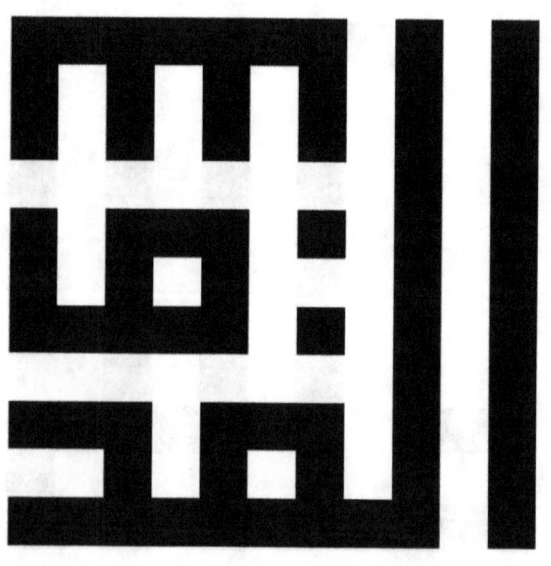

السلام

As-Salaam
The Supreme Giver of Peace

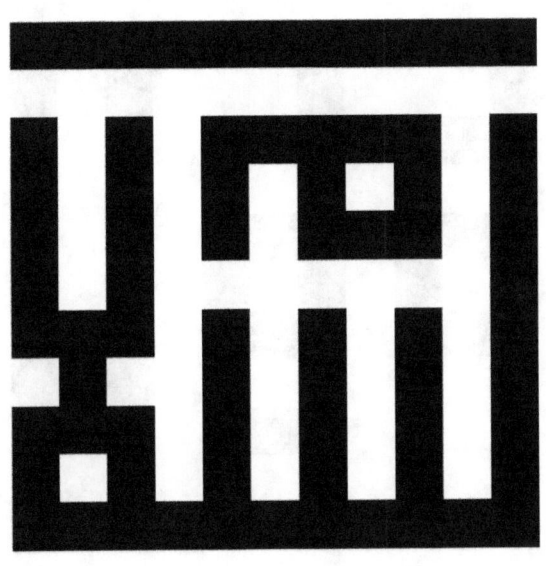

الموؤمن
Al-Mu'min
The All-Asurer

المهيمن
Al-Muhaymin
The Absolute Master

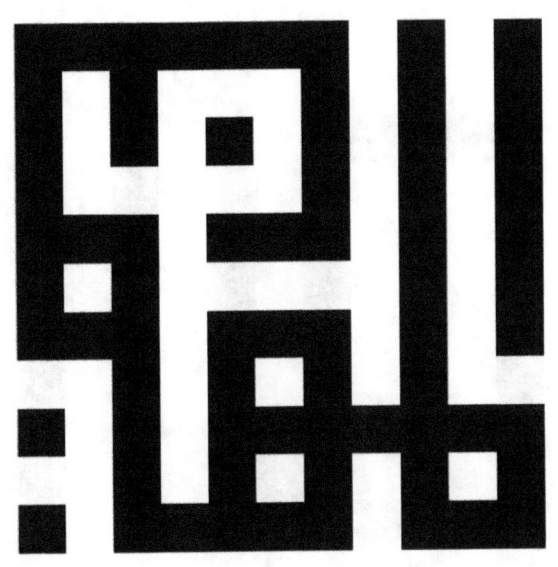

العزيز
Al-'Azeez
The Almighty

الجبار
Al-Jabbaar
The Omnipotent

المتكبر
Al-Mutakabbir
The Possessor of Greatness

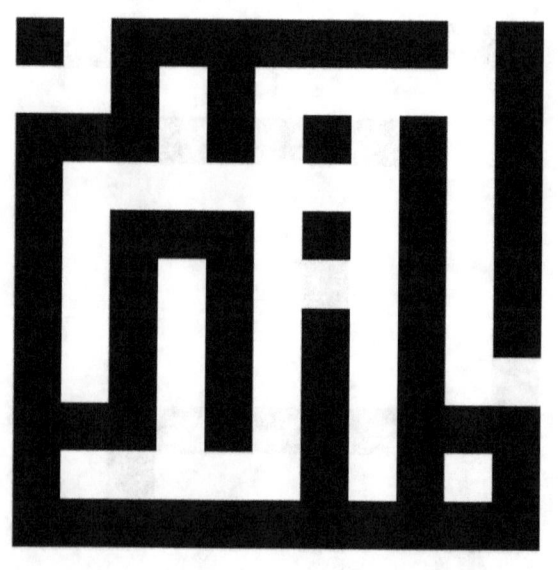

الخالق
Al-Khaaliq
The Supreme Creator

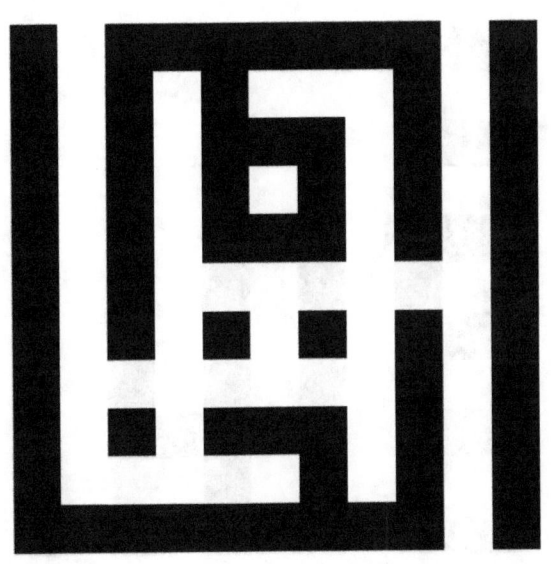

الباري
Al-Baari'
The Supreme Initiator

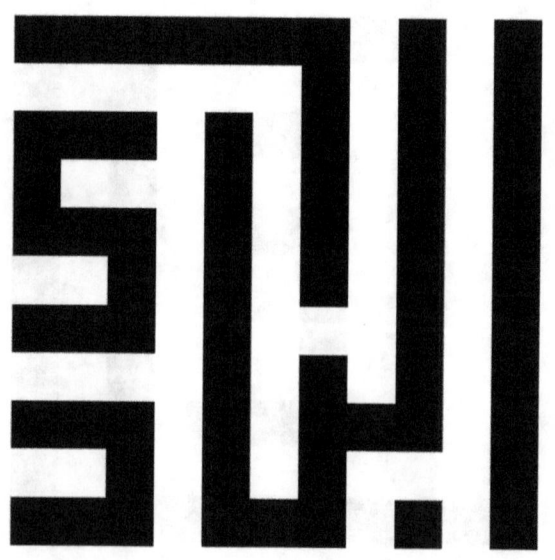

المصور
Al-Mussawwir
The Supreme Shaper

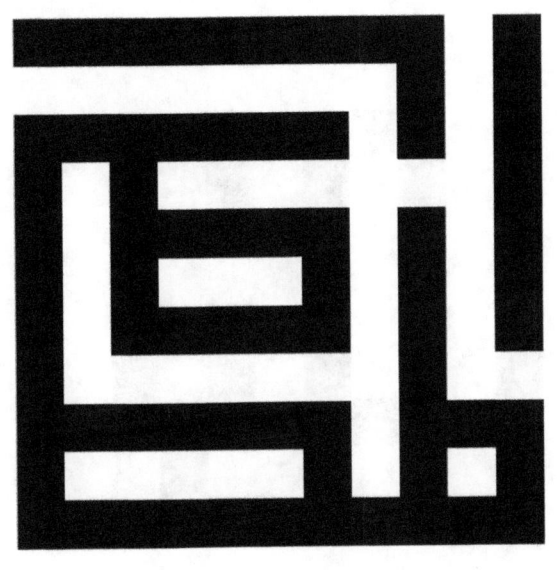

الغفار

Al-Ghaffaar
The Absolute Forgiver

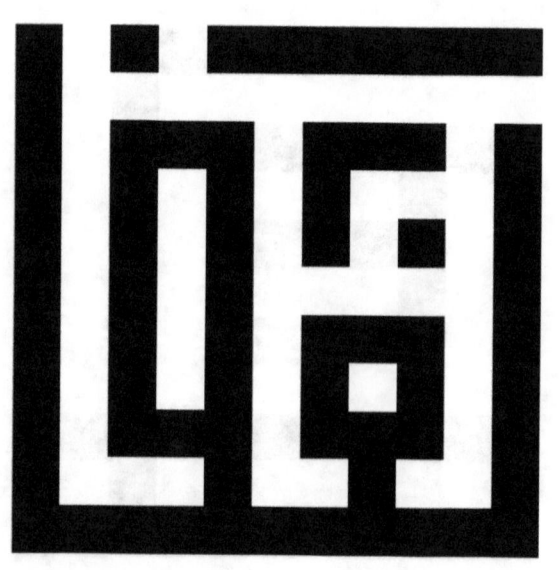

القهار
Al-Qahhaar
The Supreme Conqueror

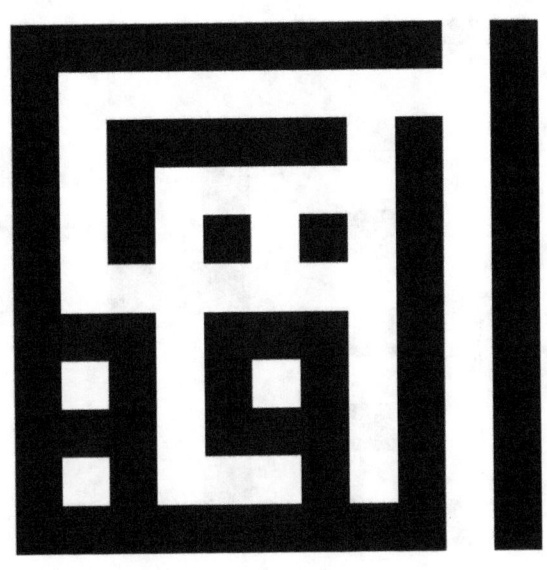

الوهاب

Al-Wahhaab
The Absolute Bestower

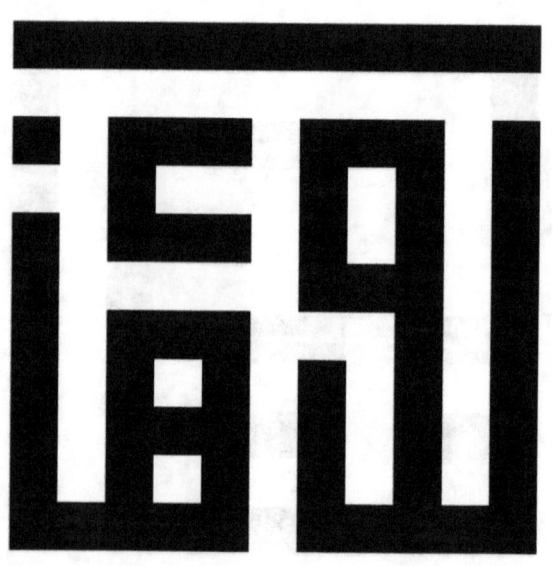

الرزاق
Ar-Razzaaq
The Supreme Provider

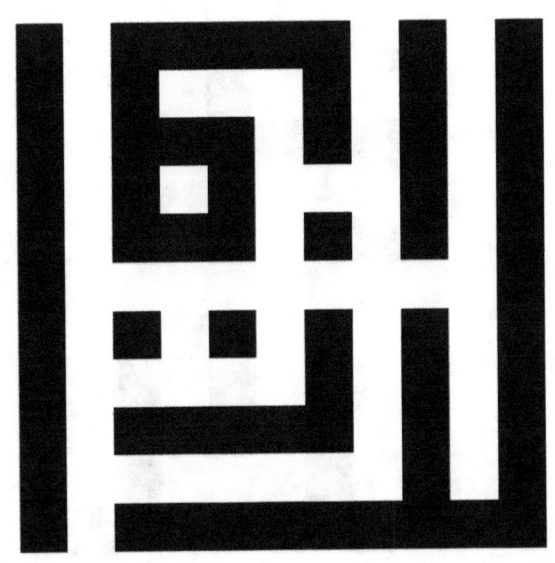

الفتاح
Al-Fattaah
The Victory Giver

العليم
Al-'Aleem
The All-Knowing

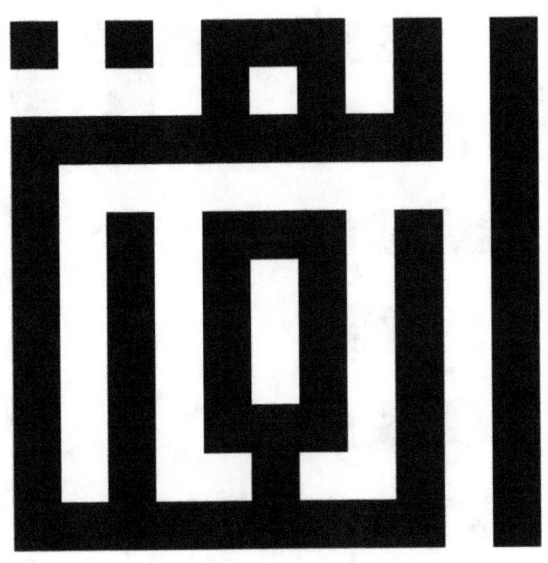

القابض
Al-Qaabid
The Supreme Restrainer

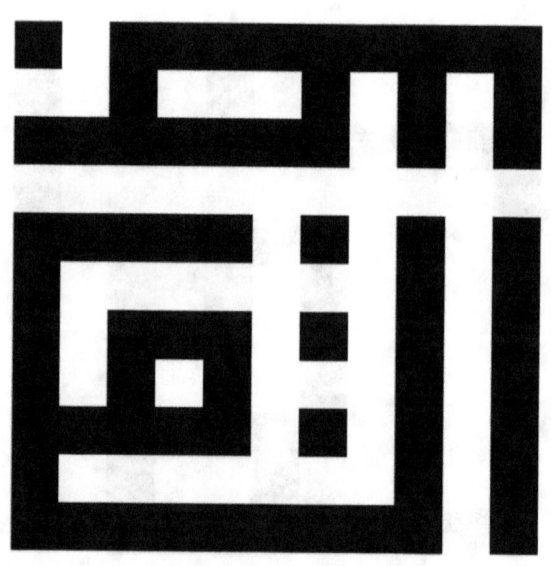

الباسط

Al-Baasitt
The Supreme Extender

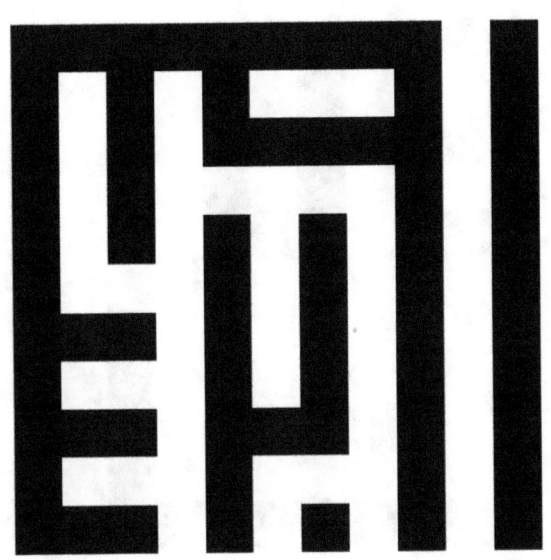

21

الخافض
Al-Khaafid
The Supreme Abaser

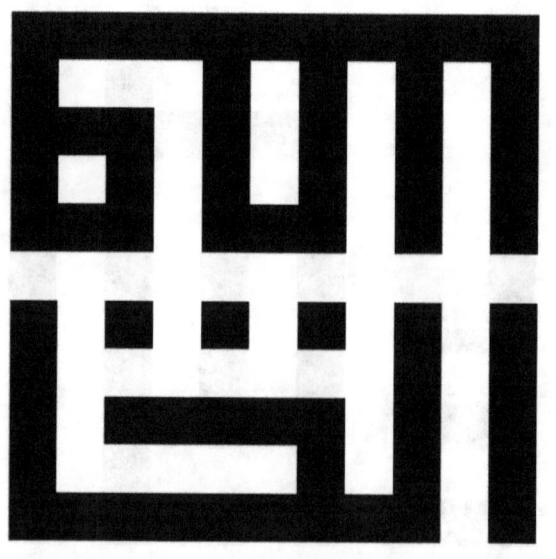

الرافع
Ar-Raafi'
The Supreme Exalter

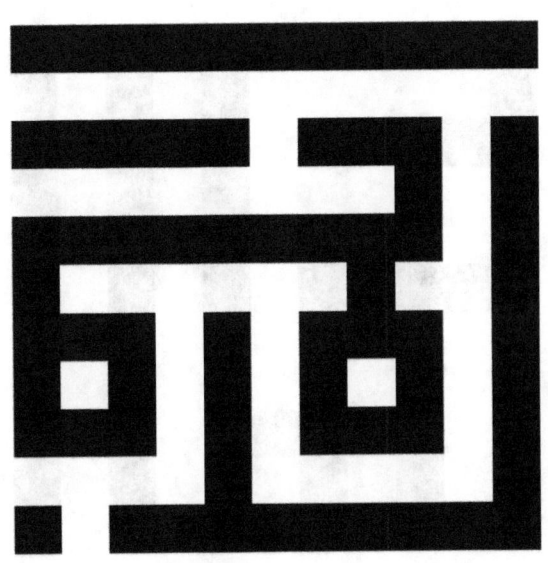

المعز
Al-Mu'iz
The Supreme Empowerer

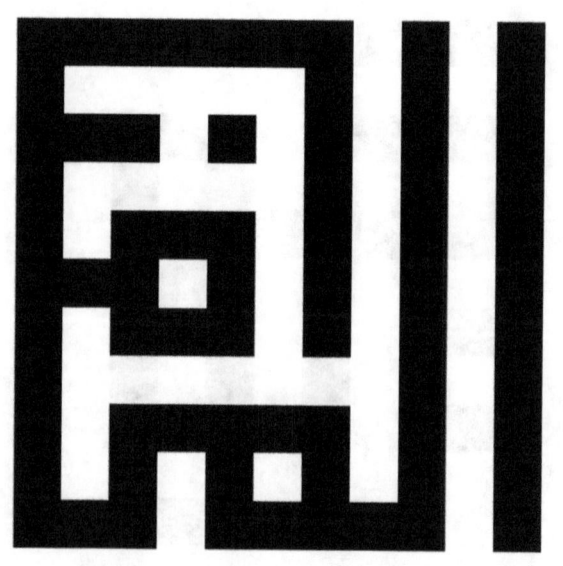

24

المذل
Al-Mudzil
The Giver of Dishonor

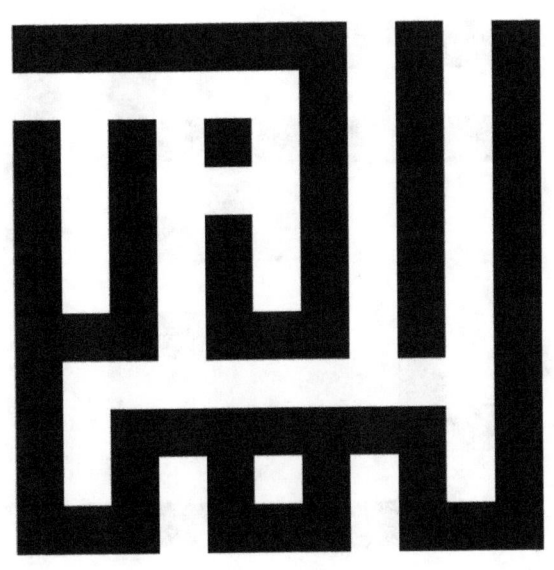

25

السميع
As-Samee'
The All-Hearing

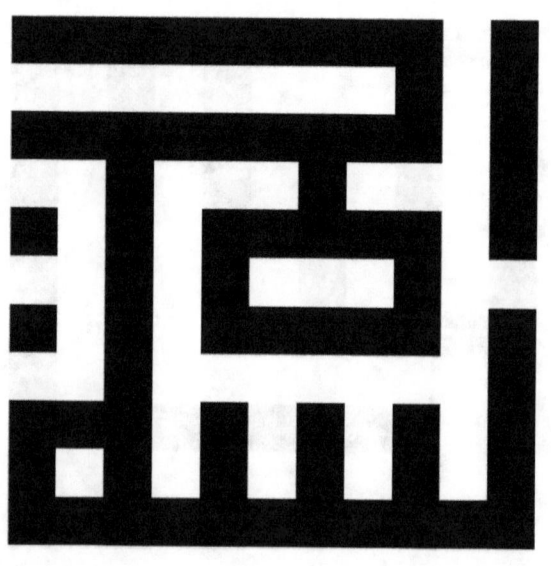

البصير

Al-Baseer
The All-Seeing

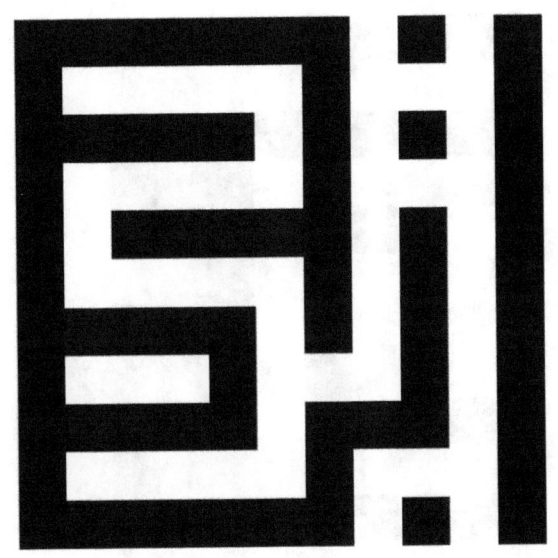

الحكم

Al-Ḥakam
The All-Decree

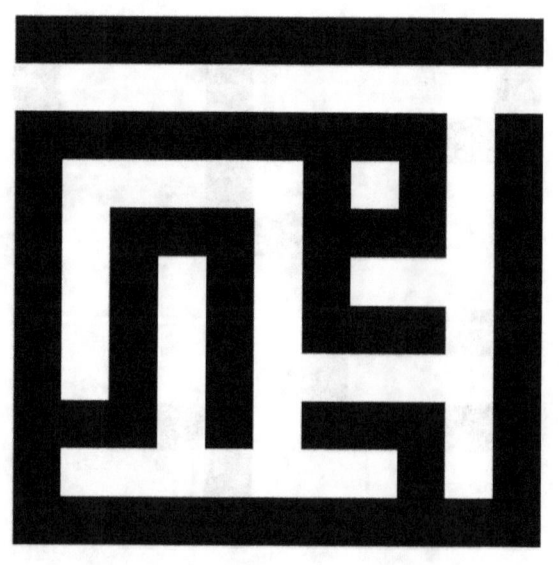

العدل
Al-'Adl
The Most Just

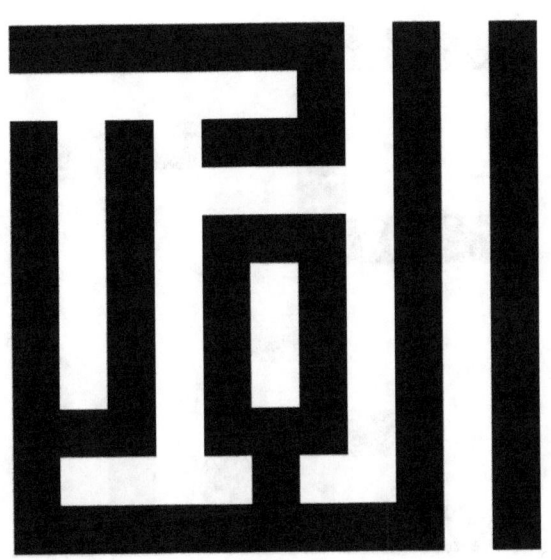

اللطيف

Al-Lateef
The All-Subtle

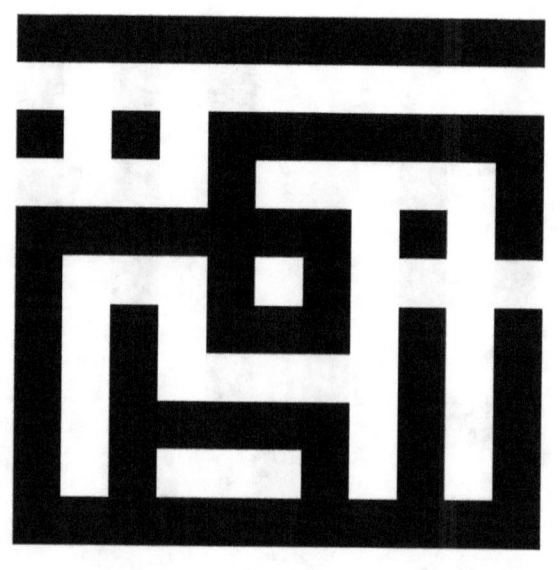

الخبير
Al-Khabeer
The All-Aware

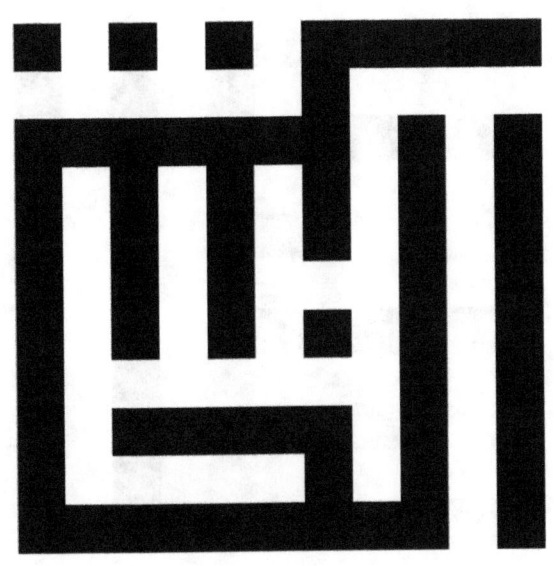

الحليم

Al-Haleem
The All-Enduring

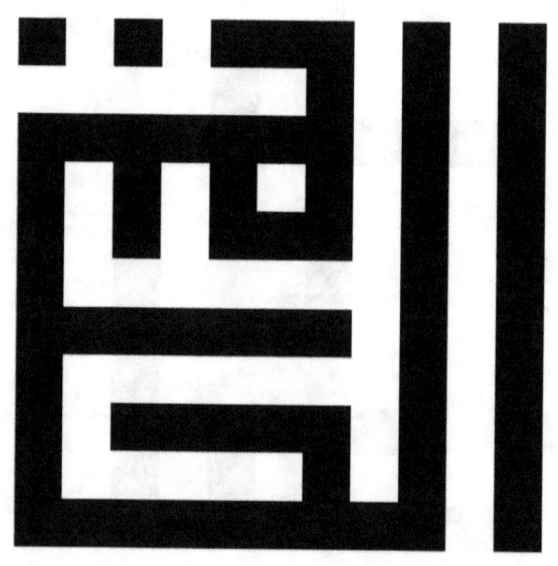

32

العظيم

Al-'Azeem
The Ever-Magnificent

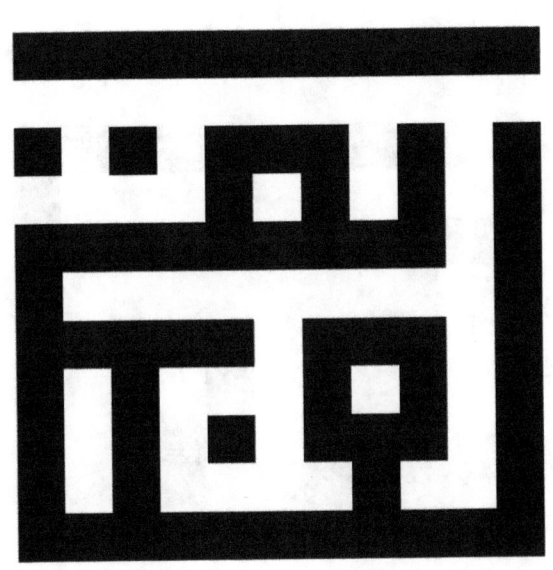

الغفور

Al-Ghafoor
The Ever-Forgiving

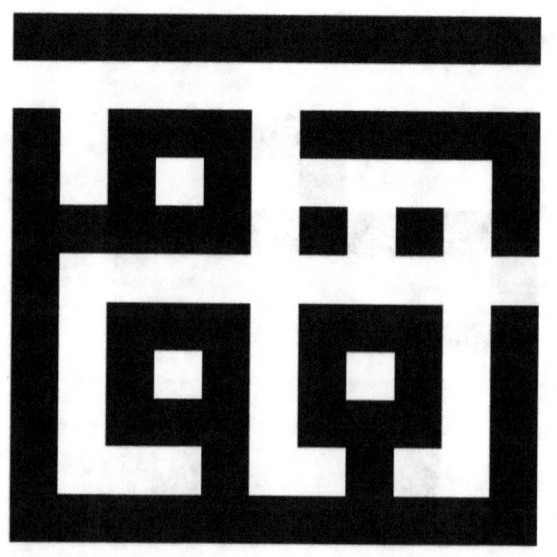

الشكور

Ash-Shakoor
The Most Appreciative

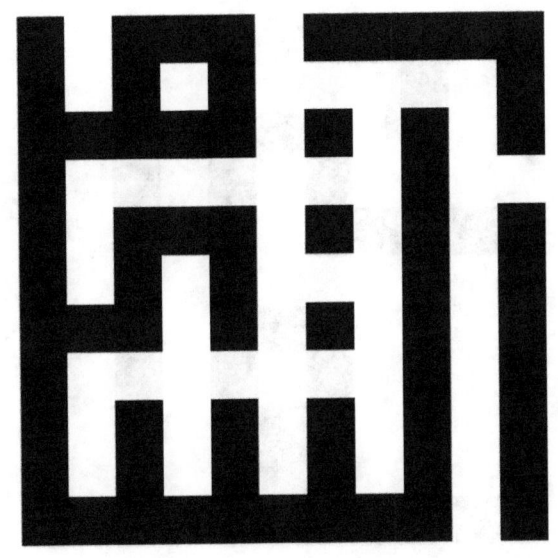

العلي

Al-'Aliyy
The Most High

الكبير
Al-Kabeer
The Most Great

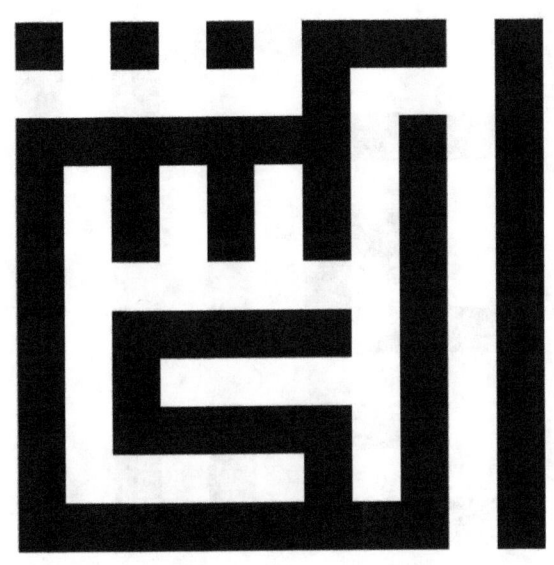

الحفيظ

Al-Hafeez
The All-Watching

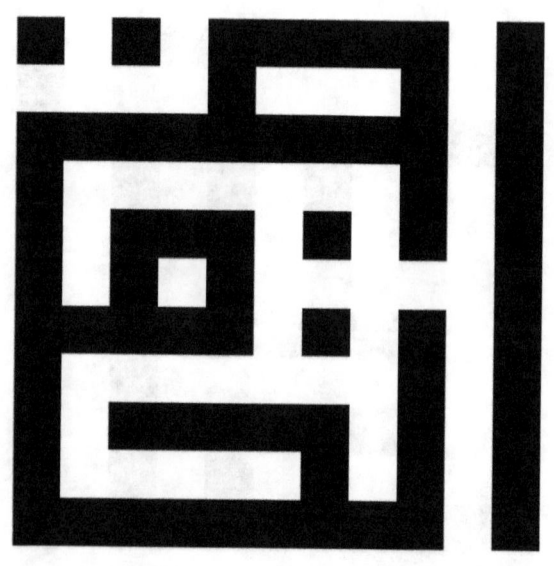

38

المقيت

Al-Muqeet
The Supreme Nourisher

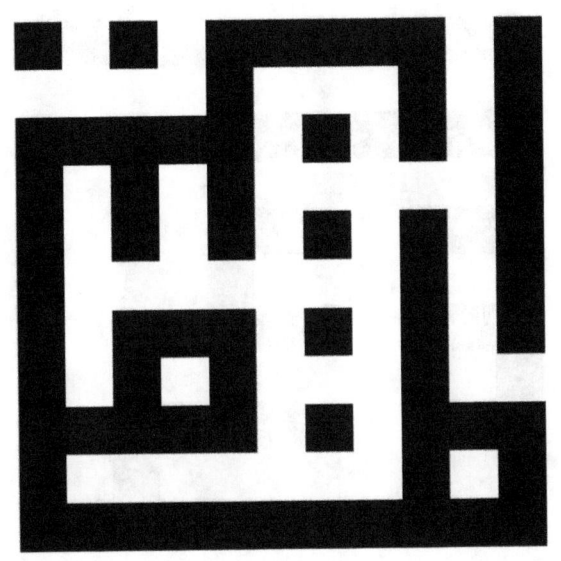

الحسيب

Al-Haseeb
The Ever-Reckoner

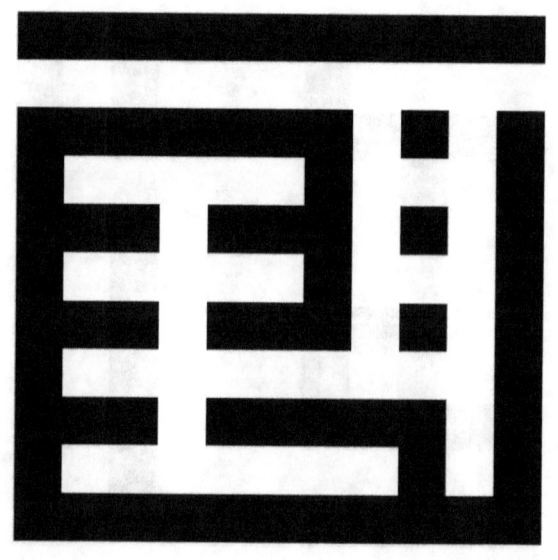

الجليل
Al-Jaleel
The Most Majestic

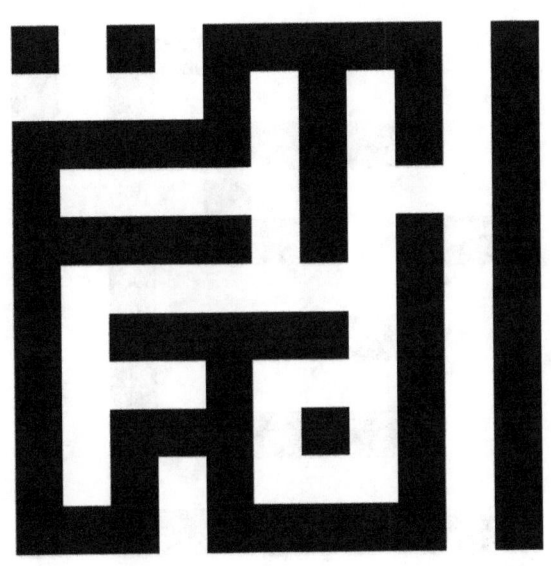

الكريم
Al-Kareem
The Most Noble

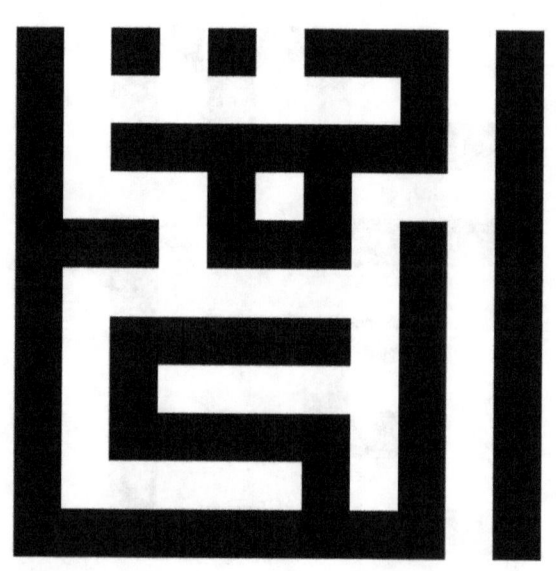

الرقيب

Ar-Raqeeb
The Ever-Watchful

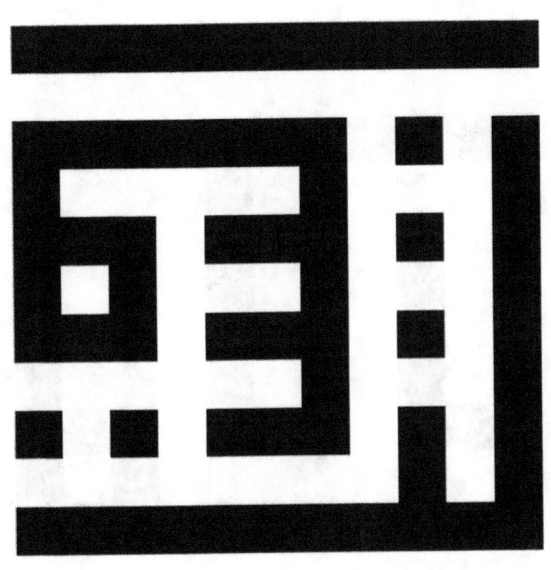

المجيب
Al-Mujeeb
The Supreme Answerer

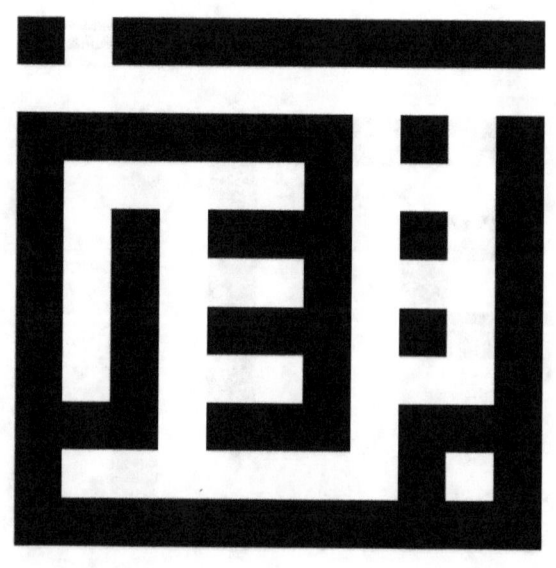

44

الواسع

Al-Waasi'
The All-Embracing

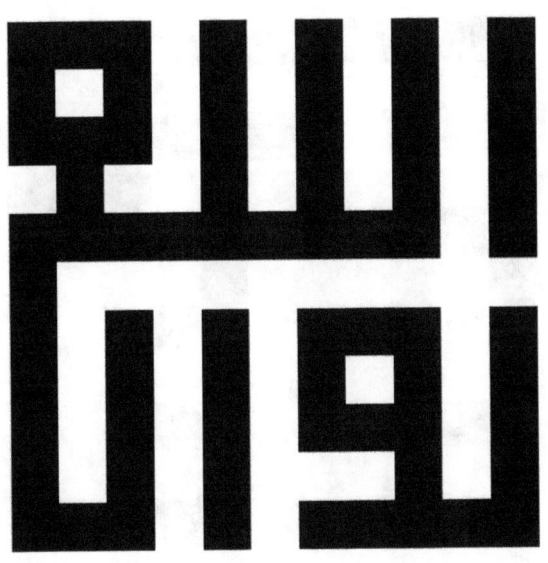

الحكيم

Al-Hakeem
The Ever-Wise

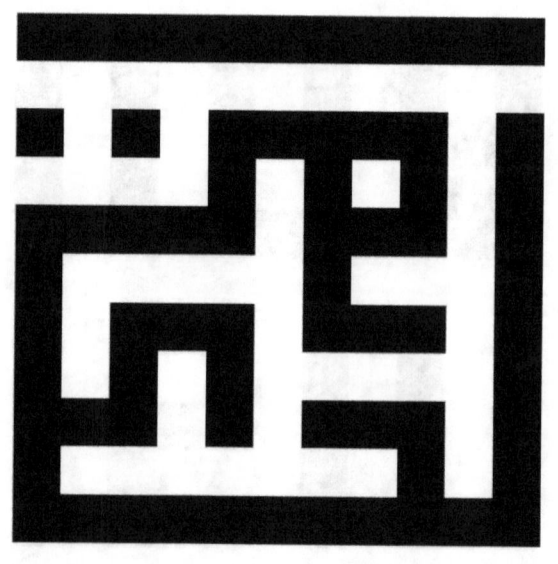

الودود
Al-Wadood
The Most Loving

المجيد

Al-Majeed
The All-Glorious

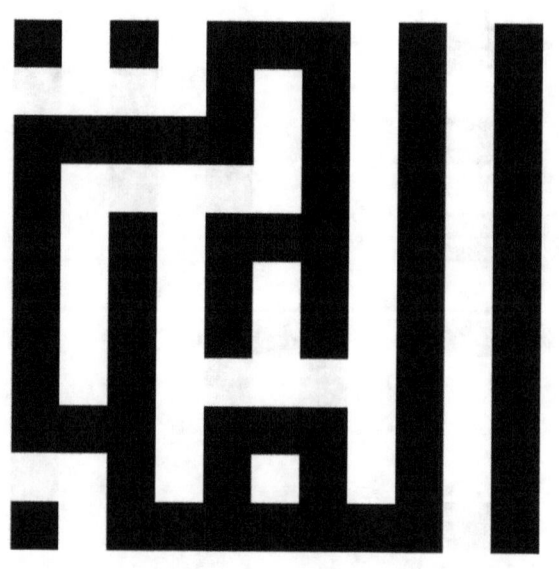

الباعث

Al-Baa'ith
The Supreme Resurrector

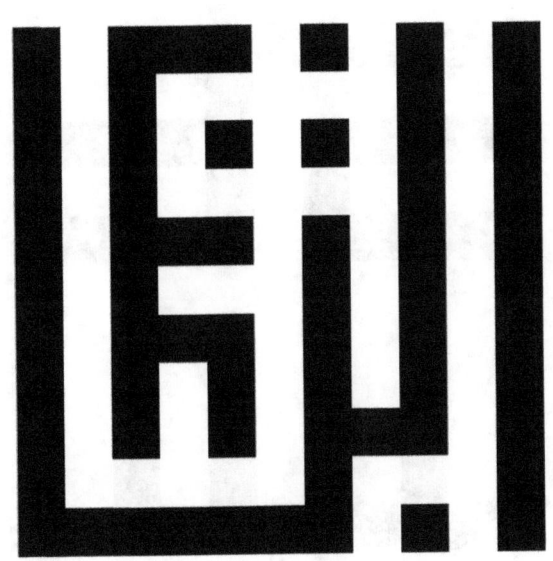

الشهيد

Ash-Shaheed
The Ever-Witnessing

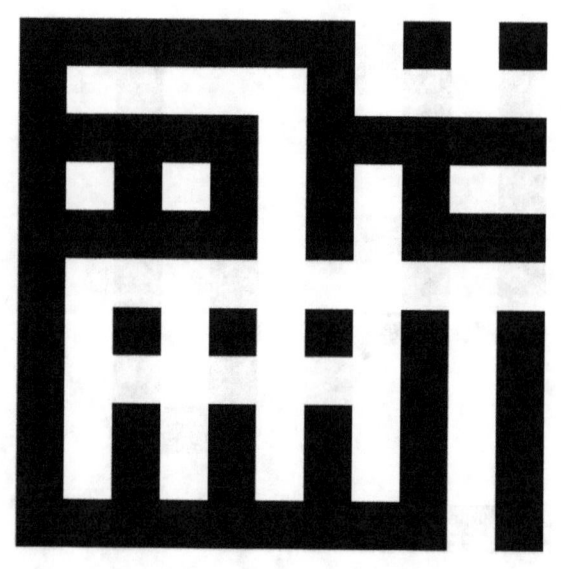

الحق

Al-Ḥaqq
The Supreme Truth

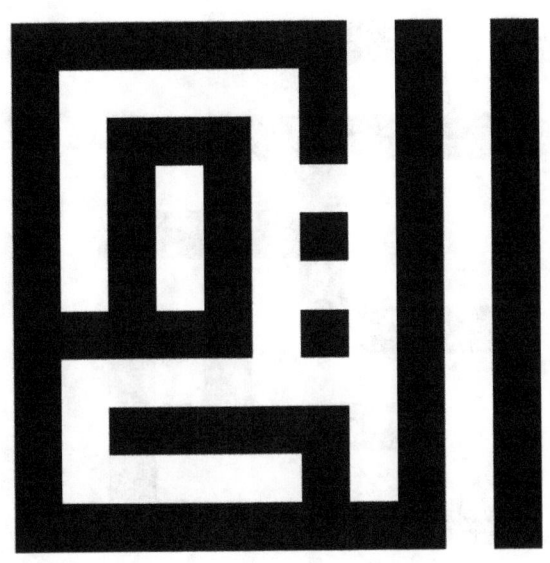

الوكيل
Al-Wakeel
The Supreme Trustee

القوي
Al-Qawiyy
The Most Strong

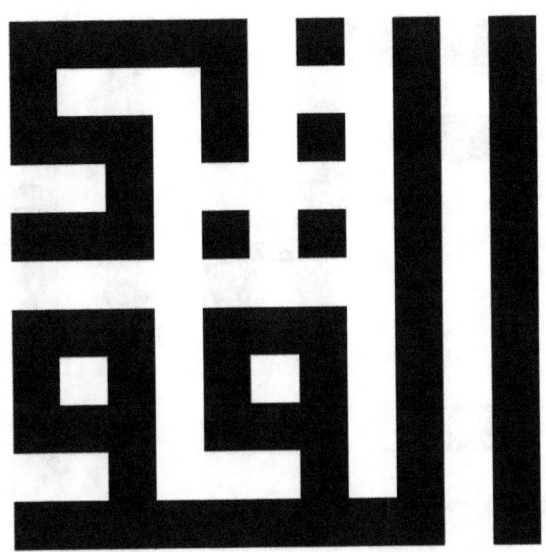

المتين
Al-Mateen
The Most Firm

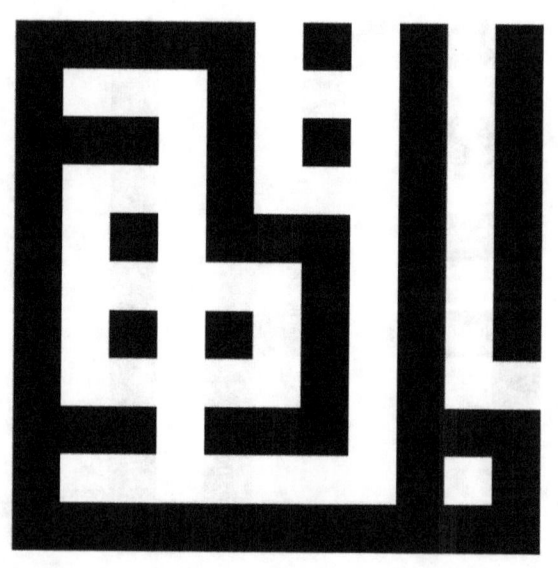

الولي
Al-Waliyy
The Supreme Protector

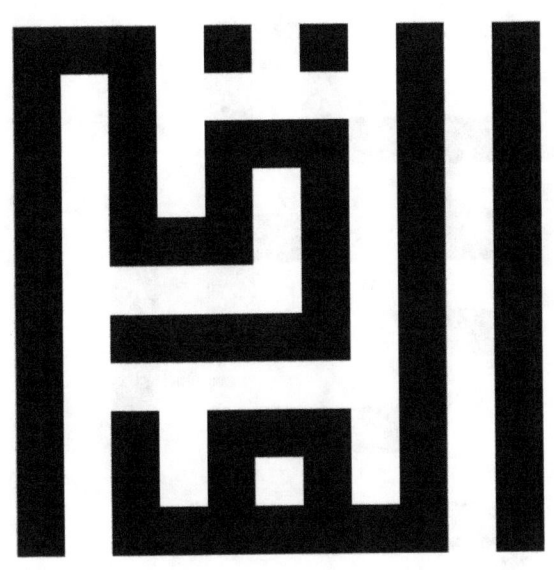

الحميد

Al-Hameed
The All Praiseworthy

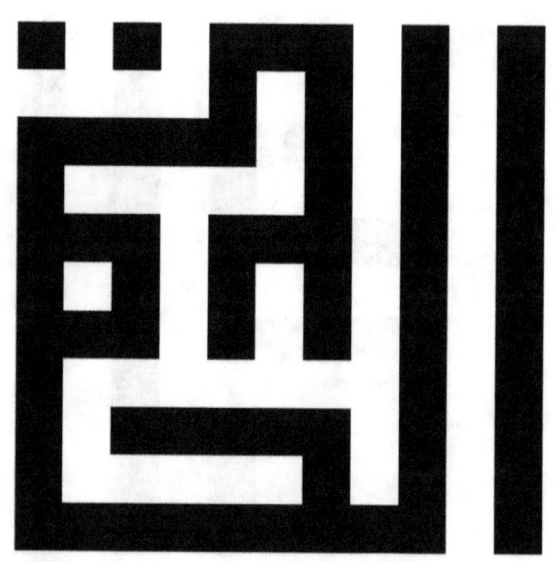

56

الْمُحْصِي
Al-Muhsiyy
The Numberer of All

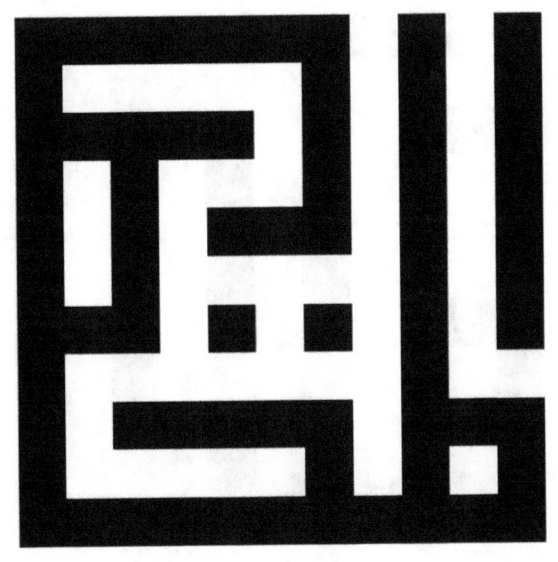

المبدئ
Al-Mubdi'
The Supreme Originator

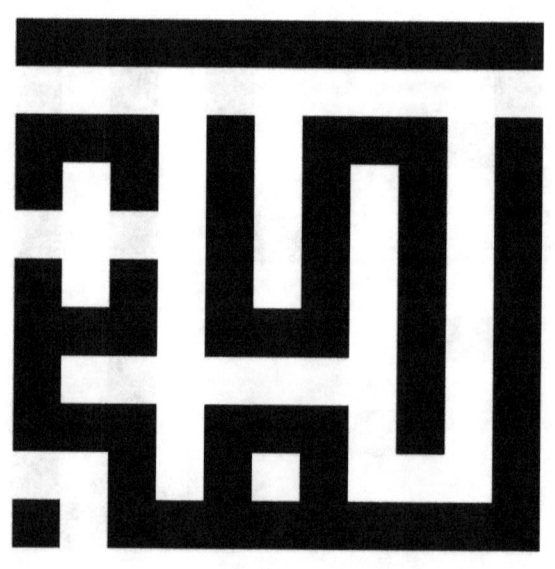

58

المعيد
Al-Mu'eid
The Supreme Restorer

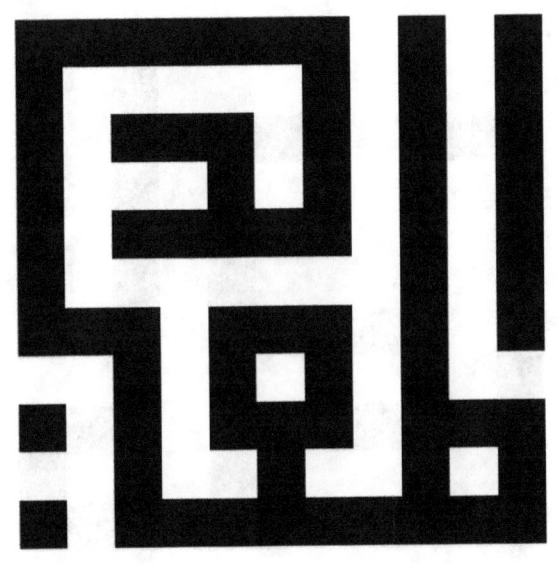

المحيي

Al-Muhyee
The Giver of Life

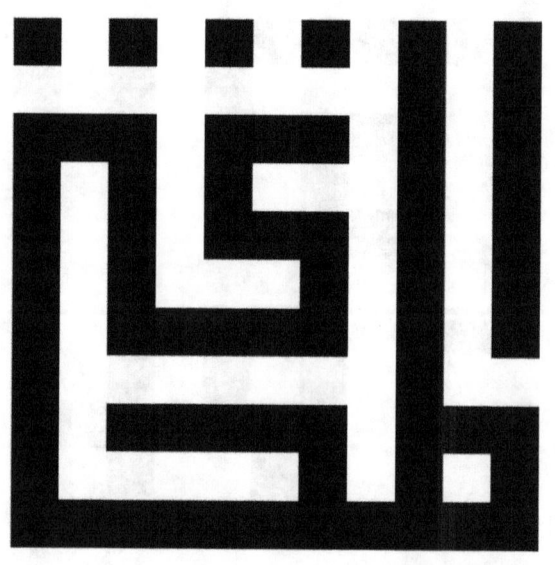

المميت

Al-Mumeet
The Bringer of Death

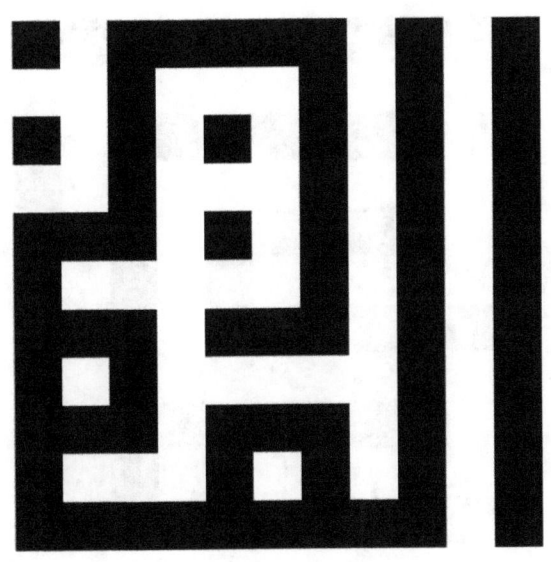

Al-Hayy
The Ever-Living

الحى

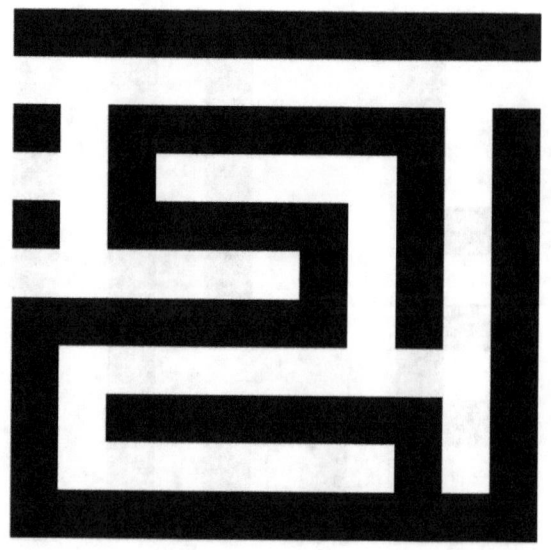

القيوم

Al-Qayyoom
The Most Subsisting

الواجد
Al-Waajid
The Unfailing

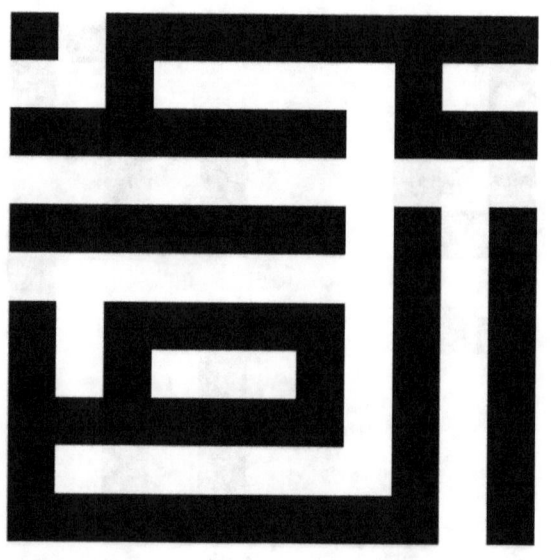

الماجد

Al-Maajid
The Most Magnificent

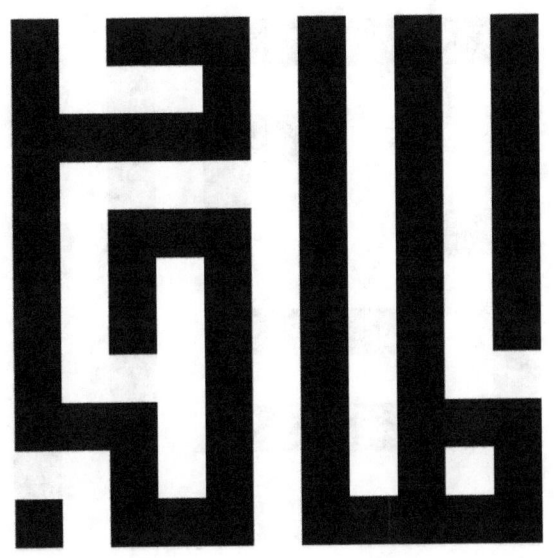

الواحد

Al-Waahid
The Only

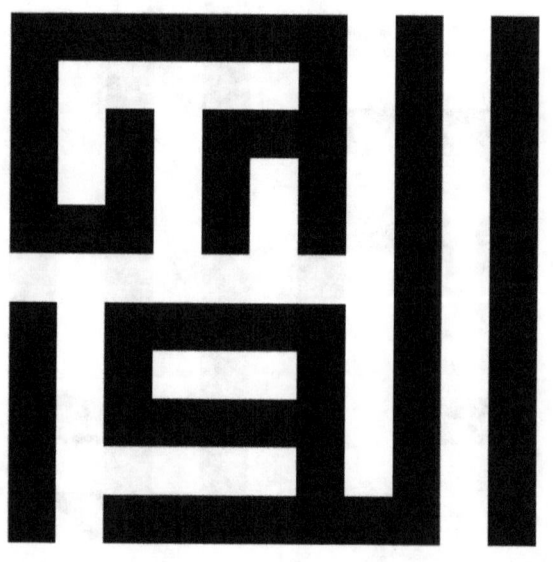

الاحد

Al-Ahad
The One

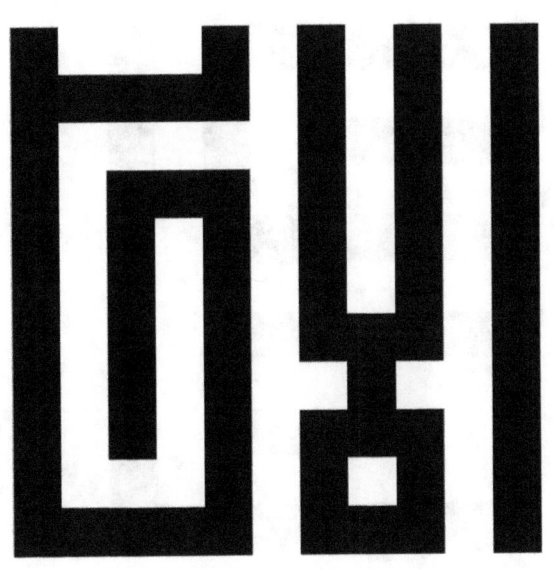

67

الصمد

As-Ssamad
The Eternal

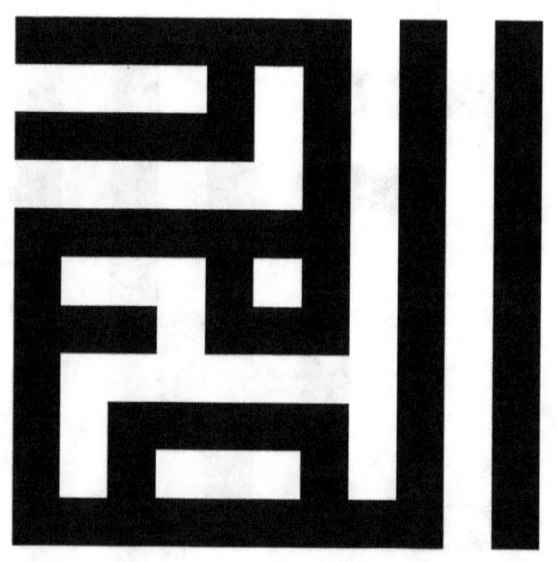

القادر

Al-Qaadir
The All-Powerful

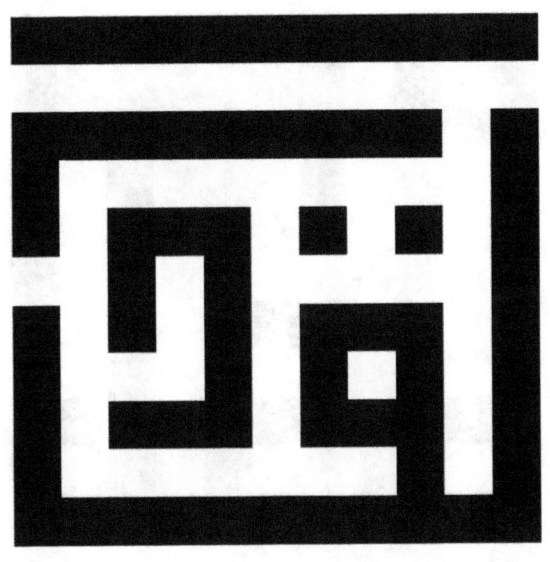

المقتدر

Al-Muqtadir
The Supreme Determiner

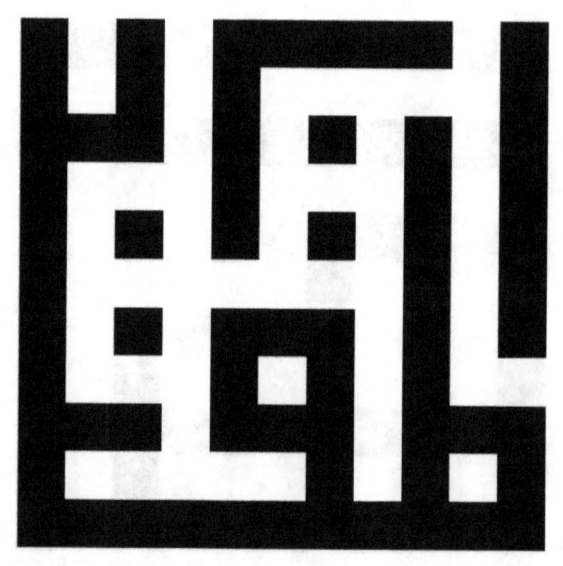

المقدم
Al-Muqaddim
The Supreme Expediter

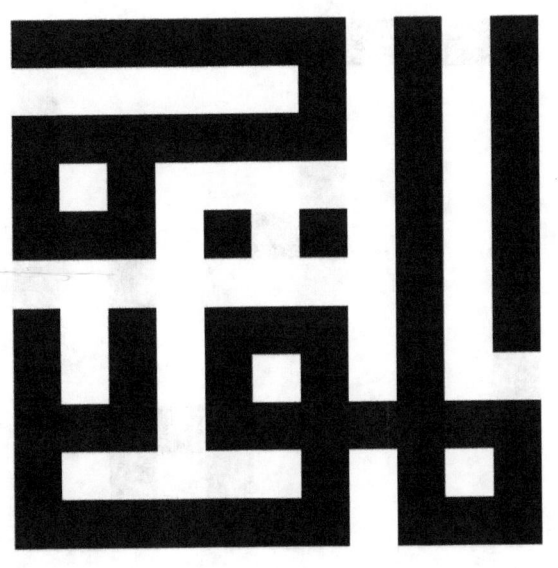

الموؤخر
Al-Muakhir
The Supreme Delayer

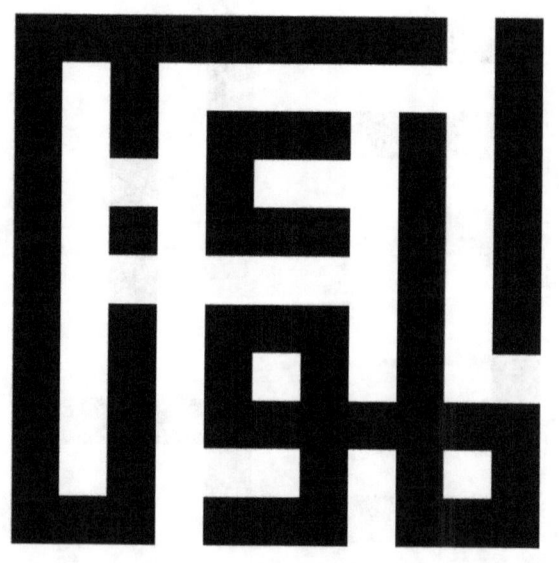

الاول
Al-Awwal
The First

الاخر

Al-Aakhir
The Last

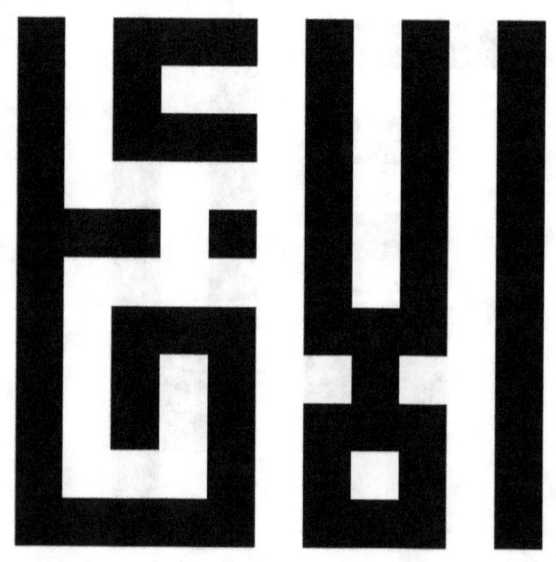

الظاهر
Az-Zaahir
The Most Evident

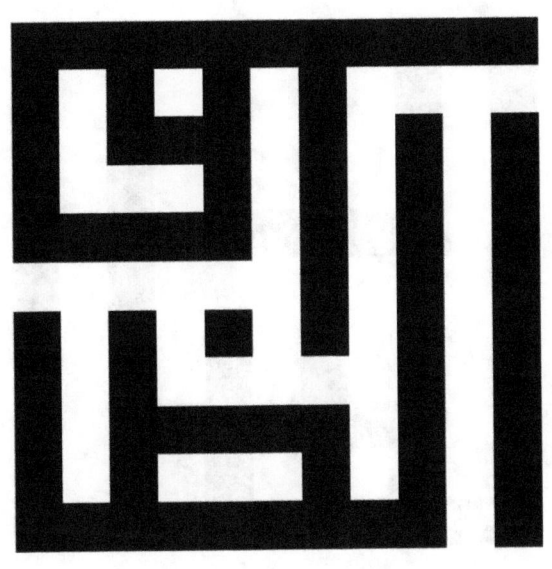

الباطن

Al-Baatin
The Most Hidden

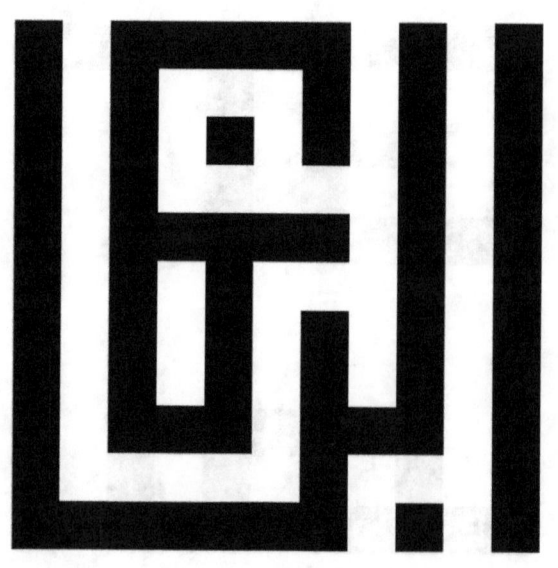

الوالي
Al-Waaliyy
The Sole Governor

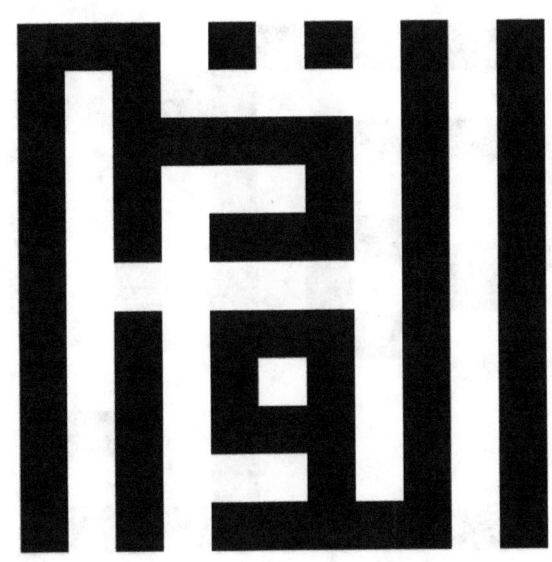

المتعالي
Al-Muta'aaliyy
The Supremely Exalted

الْبَرُّ
Al-Bar
The Most Beneficent

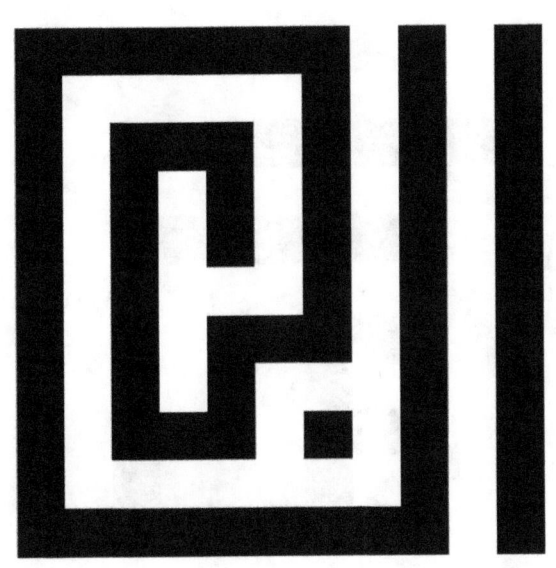

التواب

At-Tawwaab
The Ever-Returning

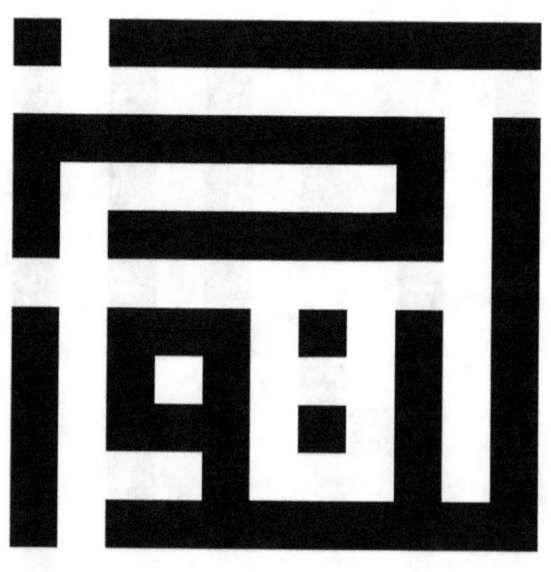

المنتقم

Al-Muntaqim
The Supreme Avenger

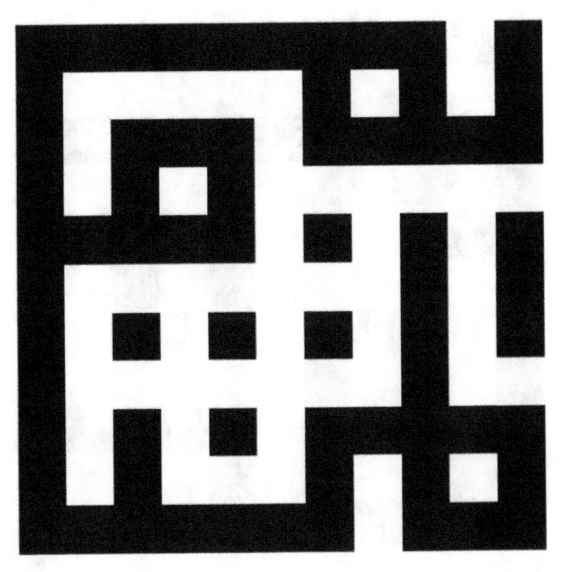

العفو

Al-'Afuu
The Most Forgiving

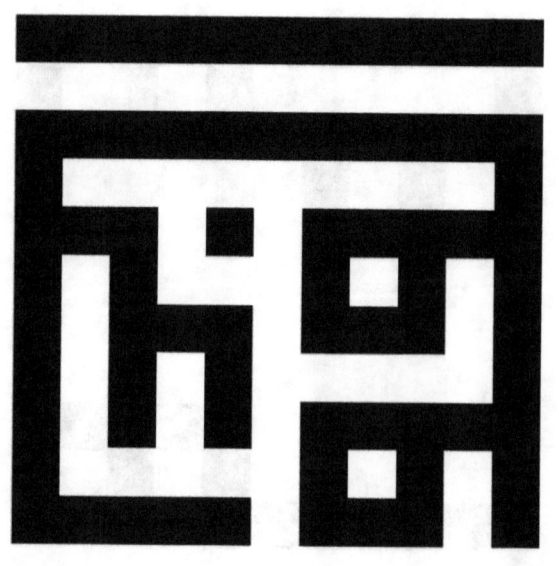

82

الرءوف
Ar-Rauf
The Most Kind

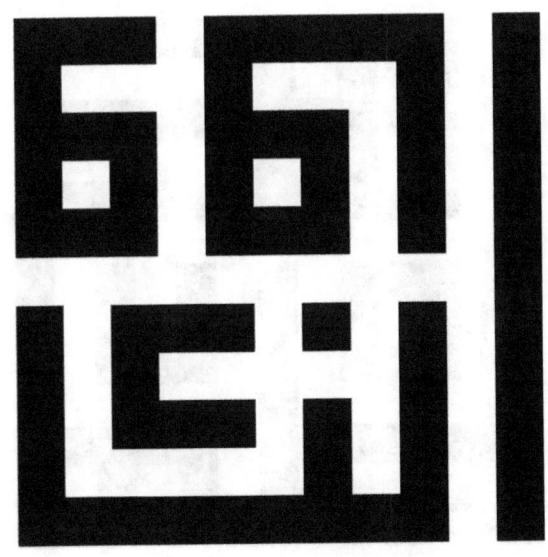

مالك الملك

Maalik ul-Mulk
The Owner of All Sovereignty

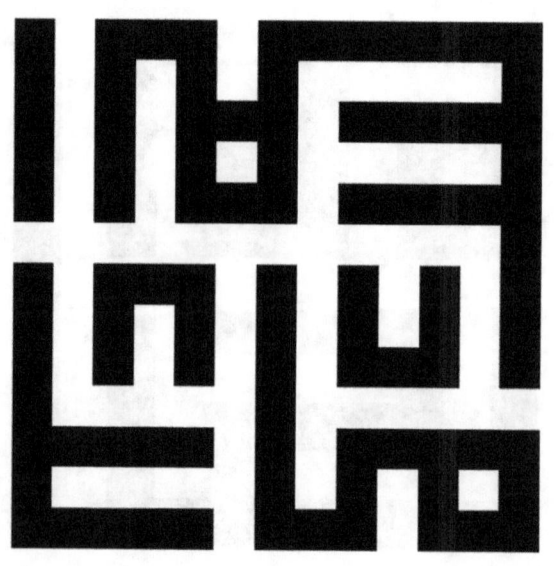

ذو الجلال والإكرام
Dzul-Jalaali wal-Ikraam
Lord of Majesty and Honor

المقسط

Al-Muqsitt
The Most Equitable

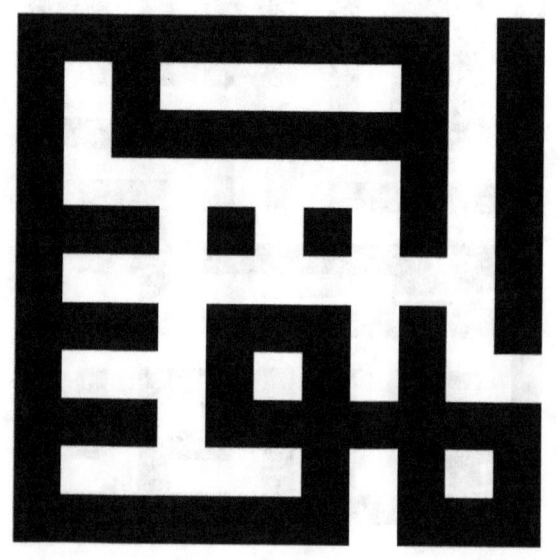

86

الجامع
Al-Jaami'
The Supreme Gatherer

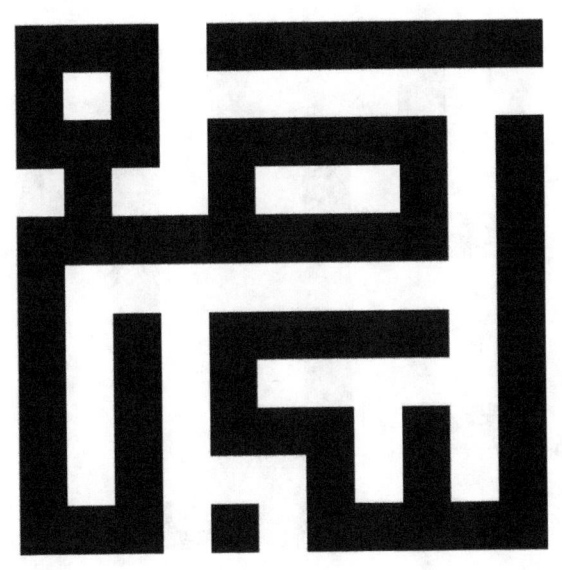

الغني
Al-Ghaaniyy
The Most Rich

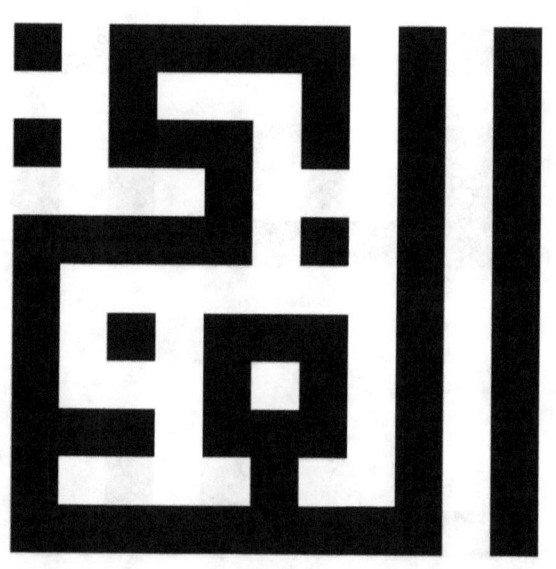

Al-Mughniyy
المغني
The Supreme Enricher

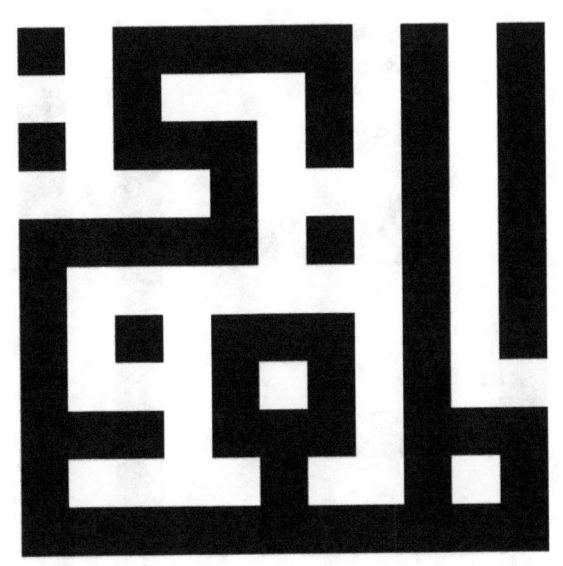

الـمـانـع
Al-Maani'
The Supreme Defender

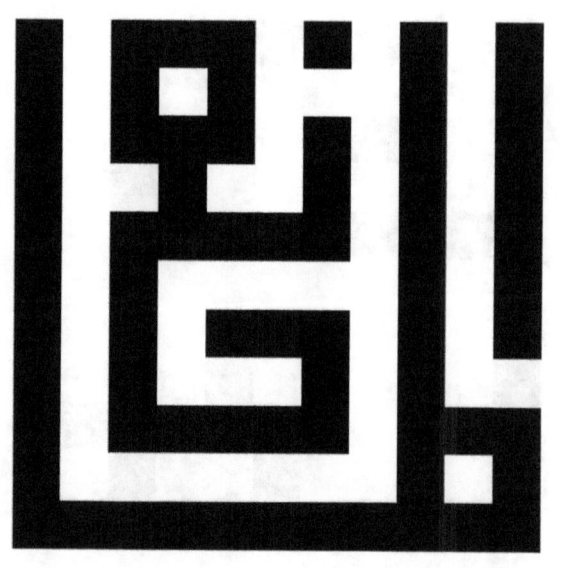

الضار
Adh-Dhaar
The Supreme Afflictor

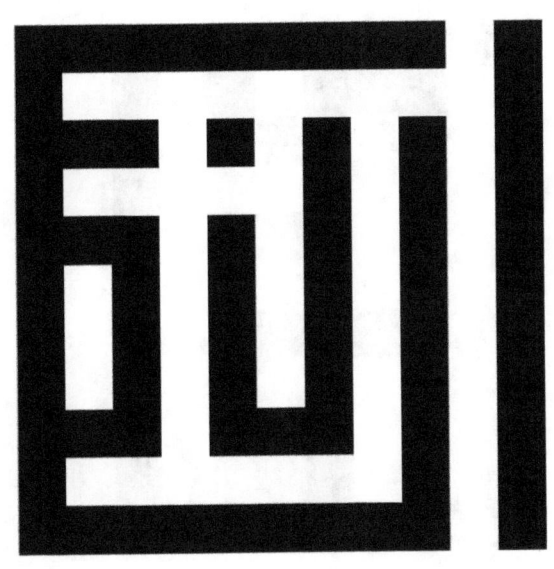

الـنـافـع
An-Naafi'
The Supreme Benefactor

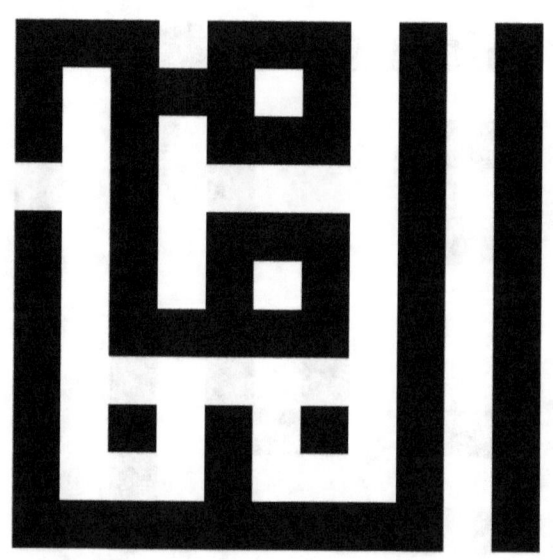

النور
An-Noor
The Supreme Light

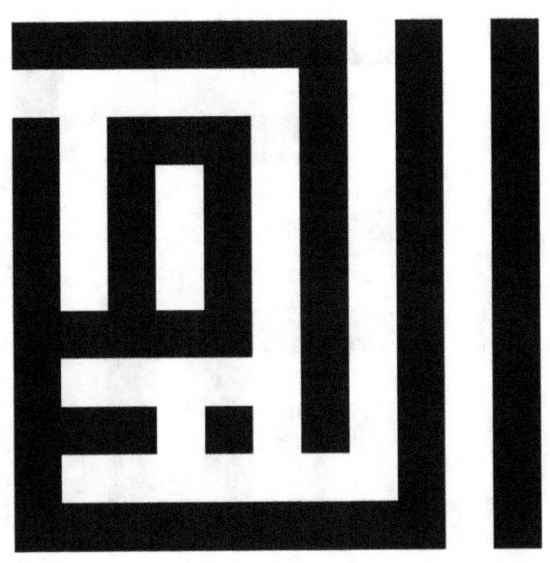

الهادي
Al-Haadiyy
The Supreme Guide

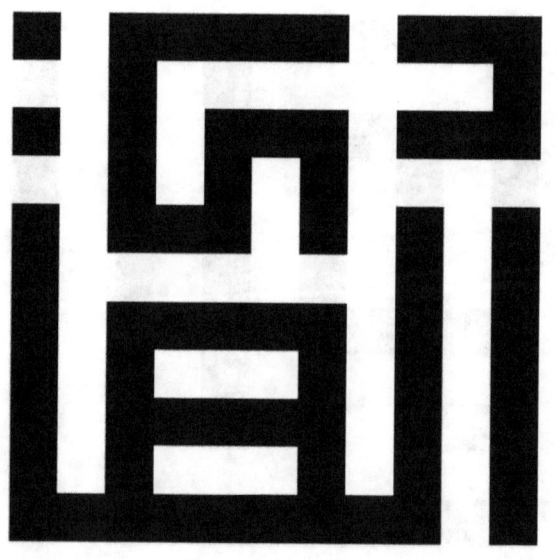

البديع
Al-Badee'
The Incomparable

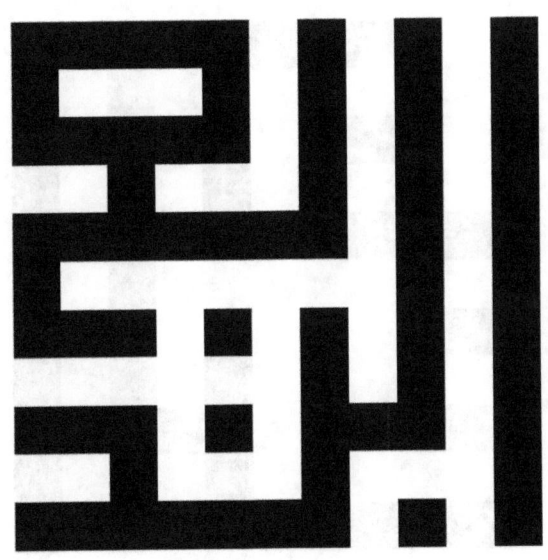

الباقي
Al-Baaqiyy
The Everlasting

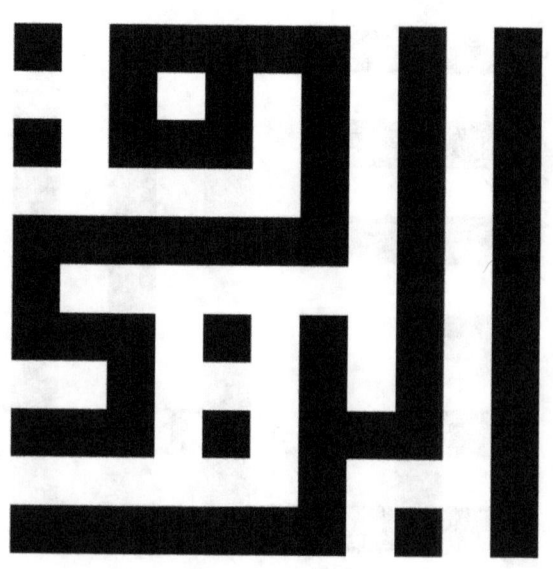

الوارث

Al-Waarith
The Inheritor of All

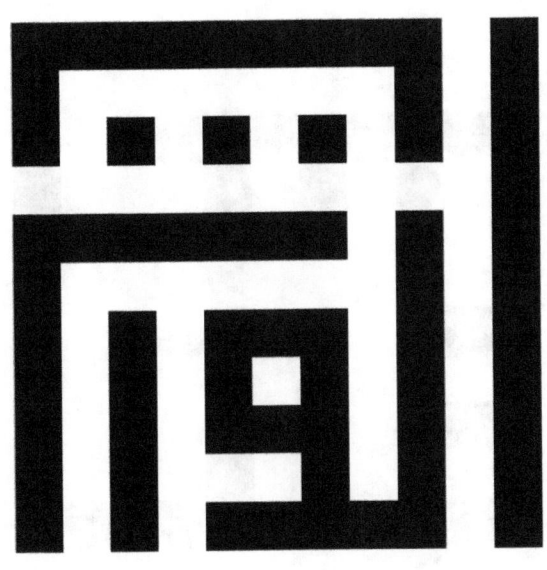

الرشيد

Ar-Rasheed
The Guide to the Right Path

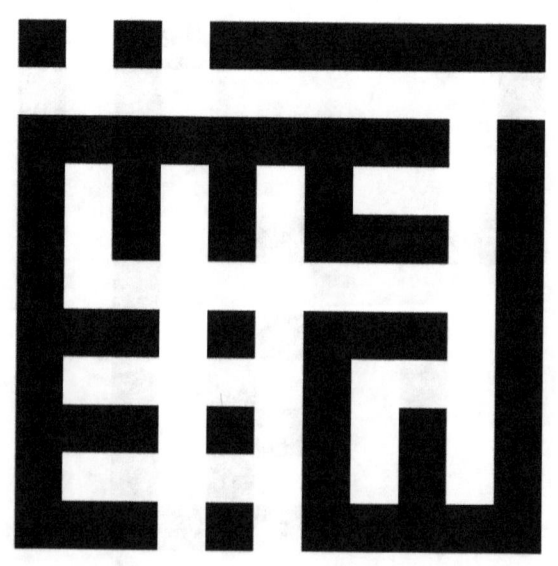

الصبور
As-Saboor
The Timeless

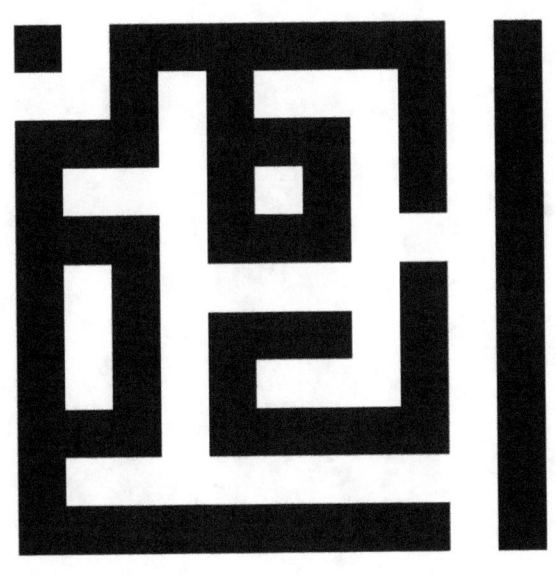

٩٩   99

www.ingramcontent.com/pod-product-compliance
Lightning Source LLC
Chambersburg PA
CBHW070806220526
45466CB00002B/572